THE **TESTING** SERIES

TELEPHONE INTERVIEW
QUESTIONS
AND ANSWERS

THE **TESTING** SERIES
expert advice on test preparation

how2become

Orders: Please contact How2become Ltd, Suite 2, 50 Churchill Square Business Centre, Kings Hill, Kent ME19 4YU.

You can order via the email address info@how2become.co.uk or through our main distributer Gardners Books at Gardners.com.

ISBN: 9781907558931

First published 2013

Typeset for How2become Ltd by Molly Hill, Canada.

Printed in Great Britain for How2become Ltd by Bell & Bain Ltd, 303 Burnfield Road, Thornliebank, Glasgow G46 7UQ.

CONTENTS

WELCOME

Dear Sir/Madam

Hello and welcome to **How to Pass Telephone Interviews**. My name is Richard McMunn and throughout this book and the accompanying online training videos I am going to teach you how to pass a telephone interview with flying colours.

Now, it's important that before I begin, you get yourself a pen and a piece of paper and take a note of the important hints and tips that I'm going to provide you with throughout the duration of this workbook and the accompanying online videos. You'll find that there are a number of crucial tips that will help you to pass your telephone interview.

You can get instant FREE access to my interview training videos which you should use in conjunction with this book here:

WWW.INTERVIEW-TRAINING-ONLINE.CO.UK

Personally, I have passed over 95% of interviews that I've attended, and I did that not because I am special in any way, but because I use a very good method of preparation, which I am going to teach you within this workbook. Before I go to an interview, I always make sure that I carry out a number of 'mock' interviews. I basically predict the questions that I'm going to be asked, and then I sit down and have someone fire those questions right at me. I practise responding to the questions during the mock interview and that, in turn, greatly increases my confidence levels for the real thing. In relation to a telephone interview, it's a little bit different because you shouldn't be as nervous as you would be in a face-to-face interview. Having said that, telephone interviews can still be quite stressful, especially if you have not had any type of interview for a long time or even at all. But don't worry, I promise you that you'll find the information within this book and the accompanying online videos the perfect way to prepare.

You will notice that the workbook is relatively short in content; I have done that deliberately. My book is both concise and relevant. It focuses entirely on what you **NEED** to know in order to pass a telephone interview and it wastes no time or content on any other topic. I understand that you are busy and that you need to learn how to pass the telephone interview in the shortest time possible. Rest assured this book will do just that.

If you would like any further assistance with your preparation for any kind of job interview, assessment centre or selection process, then we offer a wide range or products and training courses at the website:

WWW.HOW2BECOME.COM

Finally, you won't achieve much in life without hard work, determination and perseverance. Work hard, stay focused and be what you want!

Good luck and best wishes.

The how2become team

The How2become team

PREFACE BY RICHARD McMUNN

For the vast majority of people, interviews are a nerve-wracking experience. At the very least, they are something that you could probably do without, right? This book is aimed at changing your entire mind-set towards interviews and more importantly, making you believe that success is in your own hands.

I have enjoyed a fantastic career during my life so far. I've been an Aircraft Engineer in the Royal Navy, an Officer in the Fire Service and now an entrepreneur and published author. I left school with very few qualifications but I was determined not to let this lack of educational achievement get in the way of being successful.

During my time in the Fire Service I passed many promotional interviews. I was successful at over 95% of interviews that I attended. My success wasn't down to luck, or some miracle 'interview success gene', but rather adopting the correct approach to both my interview preparation and also the interview itself. During this guide I will teach you how I would personally go about preparing for a telephone interview – if you follow my step-by-step process then your chances of success will greatly increase.

Telephone interviews are being used more and more by employees as a method for filtering out those people whom do not meet the minimum requirements for the role the employer has advertised. Whilst telephone interviews are usually relatively short, it is absolutely vital that you take the time to prepare for them fully. I strongly believe that passing interviews is like riding a bike – once you know how, it never leaves you. Take the time to study the contents of this guide carefully and then go and pass your telephone interview with flying colours.

Best wishes,
Richard McMunn

CHAPTER 1
WHAT IS A TELEPHONE INTERVIEW AND WHAT ARE THEY USED FOR?

The first thing we are going to look at is *what* a telephone interview actually is. If we understand what a telephone interview is then we will be able to understand what the person assessing you is looking for. Let's get straight into it.

One of the main reasons an organisation will have a telephone interview is that they don't want to meet hundreds or scores of applicants face-to-face during the early stages of selection. If they do that, it can be extremely time-consuming and expensive. A telephone interview can last, say, 5 minutes; sometimes they will go on to 20 or 30 minutes, but the great thing about them is the assessor does not have to meet you until they are 100% certain that you meet the qualities required for the role. An employer may decide to use someone else within their organisation, or in fact a recruitment agency, to carry out the telephone interviews for them. That means the people who pass the telephone interview are the best of the initial sift and they are far more likely to meet the criteria the employer is looking for. So in harsh terms a telephone interview is a sifting process. Because it's a sifting process, some candidates don't really take telephone interviews that seriously.

Obviously you are going to take it seriously because you want to get to attend the all-important face-to-face interview. Nowadays, there are many hundreds of applicants for very few jobs and the competition is fierce; therefore, you need to be fully prepared and up for the challenge the telephone interviews presents.

In addition to using a telephone interview as a sifting process, it can also be used when a candidate has to travel a long way and the employer doesn't want to put the candidate through the stress and hassle of a long journey unless they definitely have the skills required to carry out the job. Hopefully you are starting to learn that the telephone interview will be used to assess whether or not you have the qualities required to carry out the role. During a telephone interview the employer will not really be able to assess your 'likeability' factor, or whether or not you will fit in to their team and organisation. However, a telephone interview is perfect for assessing whether or not you have the right skills, qualities and experiences for the job.

I've personally interviewed hundreds of people for different jobs in the past, and sometimes I have thought to myself – "What the heck are you doing here?" It would have been far better for that person to have a telephone interview, because they clearly don't have the skills, attributes or qualifications to carry out the role.

An application form is a great way of assessing people, but you don't actually have any interaction with an application form. Therefore, as an assessor, it is very difficult to ascertain whether that person is suitable. So, let's quickly recap on what we have learnt so far:

- A telephone interview is used as an initial sift to filter out those people who may not be suitable for the post.
- Telephone interviews can be outsourced to recruitment agencies or someone else within the organisation.
- Telephone interviews are cost and time effective.

- Telephone interviews assess whether or not you have the skills, qualities and experiences to carry out the role.

- A telephone interview is basically the first stage of a selection process. Sometimes it comes directly after an application form, but it's basically the first stage for them to get a feel for what you're like as a person.

HOW DO YOU KNOW WHETHER OR NOT YOU HAVE THE SKILLS AND EXPERIENCE THEY ARE LOOKING FOR?

This is very easy to determine. One of the most important pieces of advice I can offer you is to get yourself a copy of the person specification and job description for the role you are being interviewed by telephone for. These two important documents are the blueprint to your success. These documents have been specifically created by the employer to determine what qualities and experiences the successful candidate must have if he or she is going to be successful. In order to explain exactly what I mean, let's take a look at a person specification for a call centre operator.

JOB DESCRIPTION – CUSTOMER SERVICES

JOB DESIGNATION: CALL CENTRE OPERATOR

DIVISION: CALL CENTRE/MEET & GREET

POST OBJECTIVES: To fully satisfy the needs of the customer at the first point of contact.

MAIN DUTIES AND RESPONSIBILITIES

1. To respond to customers in an effective and courteous manner either face to face or over the telephone by operating screen-based telephony and information systems.

2. To receive and establish the nature of the enquiry, log as necessary, to take payments where appropriate and respond by the giving of direct information or by interacting between the caller and the appropriate Service or agency.

3. To operate all systems within the Call Centre/Meet & Greet/ Staff Entrance in accordance with training, received written procedures and operating manuals.

4. When face to face, deal with enquiries, issue public forms/ leaflets, publications, passes, permits as appropriate and make available to view various documentation. When dealing with enquiries over the telephone liaise with and communicate with other service units & external agencies as appropriate.

5. To assist in the development of information systems and the training of colleagues in relevant functional areas.

6. To retain and record such information as appropriate and maintain records and statistics as required.

7. To receive complaints made face-to-face or by telephone, ascertain the nature of the complaint, log onto complaints system or pass to appropriate service unit.

8. Must be prepared to cover for holidays and sickness, as required, for any duty rota within the operating period.

9. To regularly attend staff meetings and training sessions for the continual development of services and staff.

Once you have a copy of the relevant person specification and job description you can then start to prepare for the telephone interview. I will, of course, provide you with a host of sample telephone interview questions to prepare for later on in the guide; however, it is important that I teach you how to predict telephone interview questions based around the person specification/job description first of all, because it is these documents which hold the key to your success.

So, based on the above person specification I can predict that there is a strong possibility I will be asked the following questions:

1. To respond to customers in an effective and courteous manner either face to face or over the telephone by operating screen-based telephony and information systems.

    Question – Can you give me an example when you have previously dealt with a customer query in an effective and courteous manner?

2. To receive and establish the nature of the enquiry, log as necessary, to take payments where appropriate and respond by the giving of direct information or by interacting between the caller and the appropriate Service or agency.

    Question – Can you tell me a situation when you have logged details of a customer's query following a telephone call?

3. To operate all systems within the Call Centre/Meet & Greet/ Staff Entrance in accordance with training, received written procedures and operating manuals.

    Question – Can you give an example of when you have carried out a work-related role in line with your training and company procedures?

4. When face to face, deal with enquiries, issue public forms/leaflets, publications, passes, permits as appropriate and make available to view various documentation. When dealing with enquiries over the telephone liaise with and communicate with other service units & external agencies as appropriate.

    Question – Can you give an example of when you worked or liaised with other agencies to resolve a customer query or complaint?

5. To assist in the development of information systems and the training of colleagues in relevant functional areas.

    Question – Can you give an example of when you have undertaken a project that helped to develop members of staff?

6. To retain and record such information as appropriate and maintain records and statistics as required.

    Question – How would you go about recording information and maintaining records at work?

7. To receive complaints made face-to-face or by telephone, ascertain the nature of the complaint, log onto complaints system or pass to appropriate service unit.

   Question – Can you give an example of when you have dealt with a customer's complaint from start to finish?

8. Must be prepared to cover for holidays and sickness, as required, for any duty rota within the operating period.

   Question – Can you give an example of when you have shown flexibility in a work-related situation?

9. To regularly attend staff meetings and training sessions for the continual development of services and staff.

   Question – Can you give an example of when you have attended meetings at work that involved the continuous professional development of staff?

It is important for me to point out here that you do not need to come up with examples and situations for every single element of the job description/person specification. However, if you follow the above process when preparing for a telephone interview then you will be far better prepared for it and be able to respond to their questions in a competent manner.

Remember, the key to your success is to obtain a copy of the person specification and job description, study them in detail and then provide examples of where you have previously demonstrated the qualities and attributes that are contained within the documents(s).

10 IMPORTANT TIPS FOR PASSING ANY TELEPHONE INTERVIEW

I want to now provide you with ten essential tips that will go a long way to helping you pass your telephone interview. Follow these tips and you will be far better prepared than the majority of applications:

TIP NUMBER 1

When you have a date for your telephone interview immediately place it in your diary. However many days you have to prepare for the telephone interview, start preparing immediately for it. Most people prepare the night before the telephone interview, which is not particularly good practice! You have a lot of work to do, so the sooner you start the better. The areas that you need to work on are:

- How you communicate on the telephone
- Researching the role you are applying for (you can do this by getting a copy of the job description or person specification)
- Researching the company you are applying to join (this can usually be done by visiting their website).

TIP NUMBER 2

Before the telephone interview commences makes sure that:

- Your telephone is fully charged (if using a mobile phone)
- You are in an area that has a good reception (if using a mobile telephone)
- You will not be disturbed by anyone or anything.

TIP NUMBER 3

When the employer calls you to undertake the telephone interview make sure you speak clearly and concisely. Although the interviewer cannot see you, they will form an opinion of how you communicate. Communicating effectively includes:

- Speaking clearly and concisely
- Being professional at all times
- Avoiding the use of abbreviations or slang

- Listening to what the interviewer has to say and answering the questions appropriately.

TIP NUMBER 4

It is far better to be seated comfortably in a quiet room away from any distractions during the telephone interview. Some people prefer to stand up and walk around; however, if you do this you are far more likely to breathe heavier during the interview which may be distracting to the interviewer.

TIP NUMBER 5

If you have previously submitted an application form prior to the telephone interview, make sure you have a copy of it in front of you. It is also advisable that you have a copy of your CV. If the interviewer asks you questions about your previous employment or qualifications dates then you will have the information to hand.

TIP NUMBER 6

Have a pen and piece of paper in front of you so that you can write down notes and even briefly write down any questions they put to you so that you can refer back to them during questioning.

TIP NUMBER 7

It's useful to have a glass of water to hand during a phone interview (but move the phone away from your mouth when you swallow). You will be doing a lot of talking and you don't want your mouth to dry up at a crucial moment during the telephone interview.

TIP NUMBER 8

Be sure to smile when speaking during the telephone interview. You would be amazed at the difference it makes to your tone of voice. Even though they cannot see you, they will hear a positive vibe in your voice if you smile whilst you speak!

TIP NUMBER 9

During a face-to-face interview you interact with the interviewer by nodding your head and showing facial expressions. Obviously you cannot do this during a telephone interview. Therefore, you have to show that you are paying attention by using small phrases and communications such as "OK", "uh-huh", "I see", "I understand", "yes" or similar quotes/phrases.

TIP NUMBER 10

A large part of the telephone interview assessment will be how you communicate. Communicating effectively is not just about how you speak, it's also about how you listen. Listen to what the interviewer has to say and engage with them positively. Do not come across as monotone, boring or dis-interested. Always be positive!

In the next chapter we will take a look at how you can best research the company you are applying to join.

CHAPTER 2
RESEARCHING THE ROLE AND THE COMPANY

If possible, you should try to visit the company or organisation you are applying to join. This serves a number of purposes but the most important are demonstrating commitment and dedication to the potential employer but also assisting you in your preparation for the telephone interview.

Other great ways to find out about a particular company are by visiting their website, if they have one. Look for their 'mission statement', 'goals or 'values' and try to learn them to understand what they are all about and where they are going. Another effective research method is to type the company's name into a search engine such as Google or Yahoo. This should bring up a number of links for you to research.

Make sure that the information you read is current and up to date, and don't waste time reading items that are more than a year old as you will most probably find that they have changed since then.

TOPICS YOU SHOULD RESEARCH

You can spend many weeks studying different topics, but the following areas should be a priority in your research plan:

- Do they offer any development programmes for their employees, e.g. Investors in People?

- When were they established?

- Is it a large company and do they have overseas interests?

- Who are their customers and who are their major competitors?

- Where are they located, who is their Chief Executive and who are the shareholders?

- What are their short, medium and longterm goals?

- What are their values and policies?

- What are their products?

- Do they have a mission statement or vision?

Top tip

Only research things that are relevant and don't waste time reading irrelevant articles. Use your time wisely.

RESPONDING TO THE INTERVIEW QUESTIONS

The majority of telephone interviews will contain two different types of questions. There will normally be motivational questions and situational questions. Here's an explanation as to how they differ.

Motivational questions

Motivation interview questions are questions that are designed to assess the reasons why you want the job, what you have to offer, how much research you have done and also why you are the best candidate for the job. Whilst they are relatively easy to prepare for, you should still spend plenty of time getting your responses ready to the perceived motivational interview questions as these can, and often do, catch people out. Here's a list of sample motivational interview questions.

Q. Tell us a about yourself.

Q. Talk me through your CV.

Q. Why do you want this job?

Q. What do you have to offer?

Q. What skills do you have that would be of benefit in this role?

Q. Why should we give you the job and not the next candidate?

Q. I don't think you're experienced enough for this job. Convince me otherwise.

Q. What have you done to find out about this company and the role that you are applying for?

Q. How do you define success?

Q. What will you do if you are unsuccessful today?

You will see from the above list that the questions are very much aimed at your 'motivation' for wanting to join their company. Before you attend the interview I would suggest that you prepare responses for all of the above questions.

Situational questions

Situational interview questions are slightly harder to respond to. In order to determine the type of situational interview question you could be asked, I would recommend that you get a copy of the person specification or job description for the role. Once you have this to hand, you will then be able to prepare responses to the type of situations that you will be expected to perform within the role. The key to scoring high during your responses to this type of questioning is to provide evidence of where you have already been in this type of situation.

The following list of situational interview questions are ones that I recommend you prepare for.

Q. Give an example of where you have worked as part of a team to achieve a difficult goal or task.

Q. Give an example of where you have provided excellent customer service.

Q. Give an example of where you have dealt with a customer complaint. What did you do and say?

Q. Give an example of where you have carried out a task despite pressure from others.

Q. Give an example of where you have made a difficult decision despite objection from other people.

Q. Give an example of where you have taken onboard constructive criticism.

Q. Give an example of where you have dealt with a difficult or aggressive customer.

Q. Give an example of where you have resolved an issue with a work colleague.

STAR METHOD

The **STAR** method is one that I have used during my preparation for many interviews in the past. It works most effectively when preparing responses to situational type interview questions. I would certainly recommend that you try using it.

The STAR method basically ensures that your responses to the interview questions follow a concise logical sequence and also that you cover every possible area. Here's a break down of what it actually means:

Situation – At the commencement of my response I will explain what the situation was and who else was involved. This will be a relatively comprehensive explanation so that the interviewer fully understands what it is I am trying to explain.

Task – I will then explain what the task was. This will basically be an explanation of what had to be done and by whom.

Action – I will then move on and explain what action I specifically took, and also what action other people took.

Result – I will finally explain what the result was following my actions. It is important to make sure that the result was positive as a result of your actions.

Have a go at using the STAR method when creating responses to the perceived telephone interview questions. Write down the question at the top of a sheet of paper and write down each individual element underneath it.

In the next chapter I will provide you with a number of sample telephone interview questions and answers.

CHAPTER 3
SAMPLE INTERVIEW QUESTIONS AND RESPONSES

Within this section of the guide I will provide you with lots of sample telephone interview questions. Following the majority of questions I will provide you with a sample response to help guide you in the right direction. I cannot guarantee that all of these questions will come up at your telephone interview. However, if you work on these questions then you will be fully prepared!

WARM-UP QUESTIONS

These types of questions are usually asked at the beginning of a telephone interview. They are sometimes used by an interviewer to give you the opportunity to warm up in preparation for the assessable questions.

Qustion 1: Why have you decided to apply for this job?

This again is a very common interview question and one that needs to be answered carefully. Remember that an interviewer will have heard all of the usual responses such as "I've wanted to work in this kind of role since I was a child", and "This job just really appeals to me". These types of standard responses will gain you few marks.

It is crucial that you provide a response to this type of question that is unique, truthful and different to all of the other candidates.

Consider the following points:

- Provide a response that demonstrates you've carried out plenty of research. During your research something has caught your eye about the job that is very appealing. This will demonstrate to the panel that you have looked into the role. Remember that most candidates will apply for many different jobs all at one time, and as a result they will fail to carry out any meaningful research.

- Consider providing a response that demonstrates you have the key skills required to perform the job competently. An example would be:

"I understand that this role requires very good communication and team working skills. I believe I am very strong in these areas, and therefore I would be a valuable asset to the team. Having researched the job and organisation extensively I have noticed a common theme appearing time and time again – professionalism. I have also spoken to people who already work within this team, and the feedback I have received has been excellent. I really want to work for this team and the skills and experience I have already gained will allow me to contribute towards the organisation's goals in a positive manner."

Question 2: Tell me about you?

This is a common introductory question that many interviewers use to break the ice. It is designed to get you talking about something you know – You!

A big mistake usually made by the majority of people is that they focus on their family, children, hobbies or home life. Whilst you may have some interesting facts about your personal life you should either avoid these, unless specifically asked, or keep them very brief. Try to answer this type of question based around your own personal achievements, educational background and ongoing studies. It is good to say that you are motivated or enthusiastic but you MUST ensure that you provide examples or scenarios where this has been proven. For example you might say, "I am a motivated person – whilst working for my previous employer I achieved 'XYZ', which enabled the company to achieve its goal in relation to increased profit margins etc."

Giving specific, brief examples is positive. Remember that anyone can tell an interview panel that they are 'motivated', 'enthusiastic' or 'determined' but not everybody can prove it. Try to think about and use some of the following key words when structuring some of your answers:

- Motivated
- Self-starter
- Responsible
- Enthusiastic
- Dedicated
- Committed
- Reliable
- Trustworthy
- Initiative
- Team player
- Organised
- Focused

It is also a good idea to think of occasions where you have initiated projects or ideas at work, which have gone on to achieve results.

There now follows a sample response to this question. Once you have read it, use the template on the following page to create your own, based on your own individual situation:

"My strong points are that I am focused, enthusiastic and dedicated. For example, whilst working for my current employer I was successful in achieving my annual appraisal sales target with 4 months to spare. I like to ensure that I maintain a healthy balance between my personal and professional life. This helps me to maintain a high level of performance at work. I recently embarked on a Diploma course, which I am now halfway through. I enjoy new challenges and like to take care of my own self-development.

I am an active person and enjoy visiting the gym 4 times a week. Some of my other hobbies include art, walking and cooking. I am a caring person and when I have the spare time I try to get involved in community events in my local town. I recently ran a half marathon raising £450 for a local charity.

Overall I would say that I am a reliable, self-conscious and hard-working person who always looks for ways to improve."

Warm-up questions can come in any format. The main aim for you is to make sure that you speak and communicate with the interviewer. Always avoid single word answers or short responses. The easy questions are your opportunity to get warmed up, and they are also your chance to create a rapport with the interviewers.

Let's now take a look at some more questions with sample answers to assist you.

Question 3: What have you learnt about this company?

This question is extremely common during telephone interviews. Again, it is one that I have used time and time again when interviewing candidates for posts. I would personally expect an interviewee to have researched the organisation thoroughly before they come to interview. If you take onboard my advice in the earlier pages of this guide then you will be able to answer this question with relative ease. Try to state who their major competitors are, understand the vision and expectations of the company, and know internal information on the size, structure and organisation of the company.

Your research is paramount to your success and shows that you haven't just turned up on the day to make the numbers up. By learning all you can about the company, their products and services, you will demonstrate a commitment before you have begun.

Sample response:

"In the build up to the interview I carried out lots of research about your organisation. I found out that there are 70 staff who work for the company in various roles, from customer service representatives to senior managers. The Head Office is centred in Reading, but the majority of business is carried out at the 26 retail stores you operate throughout the UK, in counties such as Kent, Lancashire, Berkshire and Yorkshire. The company

has a very good reputation for delivering high quality services, and as a result, has received awards at a national level for delivering excellence. It has also received Investors in People status. I am a professional and skilled person who would love to work in a company like yours, which constantly strives to improve and deliver excellence."

Question 4: Would you say that you are a flexible person?

This question is designed to see if you are flexible in relation to working hours and also your level of commitment as an employee? It is an indication that the job or role that you are applying for requires you to work extra hours or that the company will rely on you to be available when required within reason.

The obvious and most appropriate answer to this question would be 'Yes'. It is then best to follow your answer up with evidence that you are flexible. You may have been required to be flexible in your previous post or job and therefore you can give examples to demonstrate your flexibility.

There now follows a sample response to this question. Once you have read it, use the template on the following page to create your own, based on your own individual situation:

"Yes I am very flexible and I fully understand that the role will require me to be available when required. In my previous job I made the manager aware that I was available to work extra hours if required. On one particular occasion I volunteered to stay behind after work to take delivery of some stock. The delivery driver was stuck in traffic and he called to say that he would arrive at 6pm, two hours later than scheduled. Even though it was a Friday afternoon, I realised how important it was that the delivery was accepted. I stayed behind, took delivery of the stock and checked the contents before locking up and going home."

Question 5: What are your strengths?

This is an extremely common telephone interview question and one that you must prepare for. When answering this type of question I would advise that you give work-related examples. You should try to think of at least three good strengths that you possess, and provide an example of when you have used those strengths.

You may be able to give an answer along the following lines:

"One of my strengths is that I have the ability to implement change in difficult circumstances. For example whilst working for my previous employer I implemented a new policy under difficult and adverse conditions. The team were not happy with the changes that were being implemented, but I managed to motivate them by holding regular updates and team meetings. I have the ability to understand that the needs of the company will always come first. My strengths include an ability to inspire and motivate a team, as and when required."

This type of answer demonstrates to the interviewer that you are able to prove your strengths as opposed to just saying that you have them. Anyone can say that they are motivated, enthusiastic, dedicated or reliable, but proving that you have those strengths is a different matter.

Being able to demonstrate that you have strengths will give you higher scores.

Question 6: What are your weaknesses?

Possibly the worst answer you can give for a question of this nature is that you don't have any weaknesses. Being able to identify that you have weaknesses is a strength in itself. Obviously it is important that you answer this question carefully as you could reduce your chances of success if you portray yourself in a negative light. For example, if you are applying for a job as a call centre handler and you do not like speaking on the telephone, then you're probably not the right person for the job!

Here's an example of a response to this type of question:

"In my previous job I found it difficult to delegate work to others. I can be a bit of a perfectionist at times and I like a job or task to be done correctly to a high standard. Unfortunately this lack of trust caused problems within my team and a member of staff approached me to tell me they were not happy with the way I was working. I took their comments onboard and decided to ask the rest of the team if they felt the same. The feedback I received was along the same lines – that the majority of people felt I should delegate more work and responsibility to them. Following this feedback I decided to change my style of approach and began to delegate more work, placing greater trust on my colleagues. This had a very positive effect and the

workload increased dramatically as a result of this change. Morale within the team improved too and now I hold regular feedback meetings with my colleagues to see how we can improve."

This type of response identifies that you have a weakness, but also identifies a number of strengths. It shows that you have the ability to look at yourself and make changes where needed. Accepting constructive criticism is one thing, but doing something about it is another. This also leads on to another possible 'strength' quality in the fact that you can identify your weaknesses and do something about them.

Here's another example of how this type of question might be answered.

"Yes I do have one weakness. If somebody is late for a meeting or an appointment I usually have to say something to them when they do eventually arrive. This can sometimes be taken the wrong way. I personally don't like lateness, but I am trying to understand that some people are just late as a rule and I have to be accepting of others."

This response is again demonstrating that you have a strength that most employers cherish – punctuality. The key to responding to this type of question is making your 'weakness' a 'strength'.

Question 7: Do you enjoy working in a team environment?

The answer to this type of question depends on the type of job you are applying for. If you are applying for a team role then obviously you need to answer this in a manner that shows you are a team player. Conversely, if you are applying for a position that involves a lot of 'lone working' then it is a good idea to say that you feel comfortable working on your own. Possibly the best answer for this type of question is to state that you are adaptable and can work in any environment. Again, if you can give examples of situations where you have been an effective team member or achieved results independently then this is far better.

"In a previous role I was required to work as part of a 30-strong sales team. I really enjoyed the atmosphere within that team and managed to learn so much from other members. Yes I do enjoy working in a team environment but conversely my adaptability allows me to work in any environment. I would say that I can work either as one of a team or an individual depending on the requirements of the role. If I am required to work as part

of a team then I will always listen carefully to the provided brief, keep in communication with the other team members, support those people who need supporting in the team, and also learn from any mistakes that the team makes so that we can improve next time.

I can remember one particular occasion when I was required to work as part of a team. Sales figures for the month were low and we were required to work as a team in order to generate new business leads. We all came together as a team and discussed the different options available to us. My role within the team was to source potential new clients over a two-week period whilst others sent out promotional materials once I had created the new leads. As a team we managed to increase sales and revenue by 50% in just a short space of time."

Question 8: Are you a risk taker?

A tricky question to answer but it all depends on the type of company or organisation you are applying to join. If the company is a well-established, steady organisation that has achieved its success over a long period of time, building a reliable name for itself, then it is wise to veer on the side of safety and state that you are not a great risk taker.

However, if the company of organisation has recently started up and is competing in a highly competitive industry then a level of risk taking may be commensurate to this role. If you do decide to say that you are a risk taker then it is a good idea to give examples of calculated risks that you have taken. Make certain that you emphasise that you would not take a risk unless you were positive of a successful outcome, and that you would never jeopardise the company. It is always best to seek advice from Senior Managers if unsure and this is something that you would always do unless you were certain of the outcome.

Sample response for a company/role that requires a level of risk-taking

"If the situation requires then I am not averse to taking risks. However, the risks that I do take are always carefully thought through and focused on achieving the goal. I would always look, wherever possible, to consult my manager before taking the risk. In a previous role I was required to take risks on a weekly basis. However, those risks were always carefully calculated and

veered on the side of caution. With regards to Health and Safety matters I would never take any risks and I would certainly never breach confidentiality."

Sample response for a company/role that does not require a level of risk-taking

"No I don't take risks, especially when work is involved. I always follow company rules and procedures and if I'm ever unsure of something I will always seek clarification first from a line manager or senior member of the team. I've seen people take risks at work before, and they usually end up going wrong. In terms of Health and Safety, I would never take risks. I would hate to be part of a situation at work where a member of the team became injured because somebody was taking risks or shortcuts. If I witnessed somebody doing something that they shouldn't be doing, then I would have to say something and inform my supervisory manager."

Question 9: What are you like at time management?

Time management is undoubtedly a skill not everyone possesses. Being able to manage your time effectively is not easy but there are some great ways of demonstrating your time management qualities. When you get into work, do you already know what you are going to achieve by the end of the day? During the final 30 minutes of your working day do you plan the following day's activities and tasks in order of priority? Do you keep a list of important objectives and tasks and cross them off when they are completed? If you are chairing meetings then do you keep irrelevant discussion to an absolute minimum and always ensure you finish on time? Are you acutely aware of others' valuable time as well as your own and do you make certain that time is not wasted unnecessarily?

The company's objectives are key to your time management. The above information gives you a number of time management tools to use when constructing your answer. It is also important to remember to emphasise that you are flexible with your time when needed, and that you reorganise appointments, meetings or tasks in order to meet specific important deadlines.

"I am very effective at time management. I am the type of person who is extremely organised and knows what they want to achieve during each day. I like to keep lists, which act as a reminder of what I want to achieve and

in what timeframe. For example, if I have a busy schedule planned for the forthcoming week, I will always write down what I want to do during that week, the week before. This allows me to plan ahead and also makes sure that I have everything in place so that I can achieve each objective. I fully understand that the role I am applying for will require me to be competent at time management, and I am fully prepared for this."

Question 10: What are you like at taking criticism from managers?

Regardless of how you think you would react, it is important to tell the interviewer that you look at this in a positive manner. Of course you do not want to portray an image that you are a pushover, but an answer along the following lines would be acceptable:

"Whilst working for my current employer, a situation arose where I was criticised for a mistake. At the time of the criticism I felt disappointed in my own performance, but knew it was important to learn from my mistake and improve for next time. I understand that not everybody is perfect and when we make mistakes it is the ability to move on and improve for next time that is important. I spoke with my line manager after the mistake was made, apologised and made certain I improved my performance in that particular area."

The above type of response identifies that you have the ability to accept criticism but also that you are sensitive to it too. Nobody likes criticism of any kind but in this response you have shown that you did not get angry, defensive or arrogant but instead you turned a negative situation into a positive one.

Question 11: How would you resolve a dispute with a work colleague?

Everybody has disputes with colleagues at some point in their career so it is not wise to say that you've never had one. You may get on with the majority of people most of the time but it is good to say that you had an issue with a colleague years ago and describe how it was resolved. You could state that you were the one who initiated the resolution by talking to the other person to try to clear the air. This is a good opportunity to demonstrate you have good communication skills and are prepared to listen to what others have to say.

Maybe you took the colleague's comments onboard and agreed a way forward? It is a good idea to show that you are able to resolve issues with other colleagues without involving senior or line managers. However, if the dispute was in contravention to the company's policies on bullying or harassment then you would feel it was important to report the incident to your line manager.

"The first thing I would do is try to arrange a meeting with them; somewhere out of the way of any distractions, and in private. I would ask them if we could both search for ways to resolve our differences, with a view to possibly becoming friends or at the very least amicable work colleagues. It is only natural that we cannot get along with everybody; however, whilst at work we should put our differences aside and work towards the company objectives. I would do all that was in my power to resolve any conflict and I would never allow it to deter from my professionalism."

Question 12: What would you do if you witnessed a work colleague being bullied or harassed?

There is only one correct answer to this type of question, and that is you must take action to stop it from occurring. If you cannot stop it then you should inform your line manager immediately. Make sure you say that you would follow company policy and always try to be sensitive to the needs of the person who is being bullied. You would probably need to take the time to talk to the person who is on the receiving end of such behaviour, and support/comfort them. Dependant on their wishes, you would consider informing their line manager.

It is important to say to the interviewer that you would read the company's policy on bullying and harassment. If you can obtain of copy of this before the interview, then it is good practice to read it. Always remember that this type of behaviour is not tolerated, both in society and in employment. The employer has a responsibility under law to prevent such behaviour. To read more guidance about how to deal with bullying and harassment in the workplace, please visit:

HTTP://WWW.ACAS.GOV.UK

"To begin with, I would certainly take some form of action. Bullying or harassment should never be tolerated in the workplace. I would make

sure that I am conversant with the company's policy before taking action. However, I would do all that I could to stop the inappropriate behaviour, and that might involve informing a senior manager. I would speak to the person who was being bullied or harassed and do all that I could to support them. Sometimes those people who are acting as the bully do not realise what they are doing, and the impact of their actions. Therefore it is important to challenge the person who is carrying out the inappropriate behaviour."

Question 13: Have you ever held a position that wasn't right for you?

The only right answer for this kind of question is 'no'. The problem with answering it with a yes is that you would have to explain how you ended up getting a job that wasn't right for you in the first place! Don't give the interviewer any reason to think that the job you are applying for is either out of your depth or wrong for you.

"No I have never been in that position. I am always very careful about the jobs that I apply for. I don't believe it would be fair on either myself or the company I was applying to join if I got a job that wasn't right for me. For instance, I know that this job is the right one for me. I have carried out extensive research into this role and also visited the company prior to the interview to ensure that, if I am successful today, then I will be both good at the job and good for the organisation."

Question 14: Where do you see yourself in five years time?

This is an extremely common question during telephone interviews. Be careful how you answer this one though. I have been on interview panels where people say 'I don't know, I'll see what happens.' This is not a very good response to this question and displays a lack of ambition and drive.

I have also been on interview panels where people have given responses such as:

"I want to be sat in your seat doing your job."

Whilst I don't disbelieve them I feel that this type of response displays arrogance rather than confidence.

Try to structure your answer in a way that shows you are positive about the future but not overconfident. A good answer to use might be along the following lines:

"I believe I am the right person for this job. If successful I would like to further develop my skills and knowledge by initially learning all I can about the role and the organisation. I would also like to enrol on an educational programme in order to develop my skills and work towards a higher position within the company. Above all I will be looking to have developed both personally and professionally during that time."

Question 15: If you are successful at this telephone interview, and you progress to getting the job permanently, how long do you plan staying with our company?

When responding to this question you need to imply that you intend on staying with the company for a long time. It is pointless an organisation investing time, effort and resources into your training and development if you do not plan on staying with them. You have identified that this is the company you want to work for, and therefore you want to commit your future to them.

All the time you are contributing effectively towards the company's desired achievements then you will be a part of them. If you say that you only plan to stay with them for a few years before moving on then they are unlikely to employ you. They want to know that they are going to get a substantial return for their investment.

"I have looked into both this role and the organisation. I have been impressed with the ambitions and plans that the company have. With that in mind I plan to stay with you for a long time if I am successful. Furthermore, I am serious about my application for this position and excited about the prospect of working with you. I understand that you are going to be investing a lot of time, money and resources into my development and I would intend repaying that investment by being a loyal and competent employee."

Question 16: Why do you want to leave your current employment?

This is a question that needs to be answered very carefully. It is not a good idea to state that you are leaving because of differences with a manager or member of the team. It is far better to say that you are looking for new and fresh challenges and feel that you have achieved all that you can at the company. Most people want a higher salary but it is also not a good idea to use this as a reason for your intention to move organisations. By stating you would like a new challenge you will demonstrate drive and enthusiasm.

"Although I enjoy my current job I am now ready for a new challenge. I have worked hard for my previous employer and they have been good to me in return. I have learnt an awful lot during my time with them but I am now in a position where I want to embark on new and fresh challenges. I will be leaving my current company with fond memories but I know the time is right for me to move on.

Having looked into your company and the role that I'm applying for I feel that I have so much to offer in terms of my experience, drive and enthusiasm and know that I would be a valuable asset to the team."

Question 17: Why should we give you the job?

You need to give the interviewer an answer that benefits them and not just yourself. Yes of course you are the best person for the job, but don't say it unless you can back it up with examples of why. Here are a few example of why you might be the best person for the job:

- You have the ability to work in a fast-changing environment that requires commitment, drive and enthusiasm.

- You are capable of achieving great things for their organisation and thrive under pressurised situations. For example in your previous role you were given a deadline of three days to achieve a highly complex task that required a high level of motivational skills to get the task completed on time. You brought the team together, briefed them on what was expected and monitored each stage of progress carefully.

- You can make a positive impact on sales/profit or turnover and are dependable in every situation to deliver what is required.

- You are a team player who has the experiences and skills to match the job description.

- You are loyal, hard-working and will act as a positive role model for their organisation.

This type of question can make or break you and you should be prepared with a hard-hitting positive response. Be verbally enthusiastic when responding and give brief examples of why you are the right person compared to the next candidate.

Question 18: What qualities do you believe a good manager should have?

You are more likely to be asked this type of telephone interview question if you are applying for a managerial position. If you are applying for a managerial or supervisory position then this question is designed to find out what you will be like as a manager. Managers are required to lead and also to be great role models for the organisation. Have a look at the following response.

"The key quality should be leadership and the ability to look ahead towards the horizon. The manager needs to be ten steps ahead and already making plans for the future. They also should be good role models and be capable of leading by example. Approachable, fair and enthusiastic are other important qualities but above all a successful manager needs to lead when things aren't going as planned. It is his or her responsibility to lift a team out of a difficult period and motivate people to achieve the vision of the organisation. The highest calling of a true leader is inspiring others to reach the highest of their abilities. The company's aims, objectives and vision are what the manager should work towards and have at the forefront of his/her mind at all times."

Some of the qualities of a competent manager include:

- Being a visionary and a role model for the company
- Being able to delegate work effectively
- Identifying strengths in employees and using those strengths effectively
- Identifying development needs in individuals and providing appropriate feedback and support where necessary
- Being flexible and adaptable when required
- Being capable of implementing the company's policies, procedures and vision
- Leading by example

Question 19: Can you tell us about a situation when you have had to work under pressure?

Some jobs, such as sales and customer service roles, will require you to work under pressure. The telephone interviewer will therefore want to know that you have the ability to perform in such an environment. If you have experience of working under pressure then you are far more likely to succeed in a high-pressurised role. When responding to a question of this nature, try to provide an actual example of where you have achieved a task whilst being under pressure.

There now follows a sample response to this question.

"Yes, I can. In my current job as car mechanic for a well-known company, I was presented with a difficult and pressurised situation. A member of the team had made a mistake and had fitted a number of wrong components to a car. The car in question was due to be picked up at 2pm and the customer had stated how important it was that his car was ready on time because he had an important meeting to attend. We only had two hours in which to resolve the issue and I volunteered to be the one who would carry out the work on the car. The problem was that we had three other customers in the workshop waiting for their cars too, so I was the only person who could be spared at that particular time. I worked solidly for the next two hours making sure that I meticulously carried out each task in line with our operating procedures. Even though I didn't finish the car until 2.10pm, I managed to achieve a very difficult task under pressurised conditions whilst keeping strictly to procedures and regulations."

Question 20: Can you tell me about a time when you have worked as part of a team to achieve a goal?

Having the ability to work as part of a team is very important to the vast majority of jobs that you will apply for. Most large companies will employ many people in many different roles ranging from customer service and administration, through to management and operations. In fact it is not uncommon for thousands of people to work for one particular company. Therefore, it is essential that every member of the team works together in order to achieve the ultimate goal that the company sets. The telephone interviewer will want to be certain that you can work effectively as part of a team, which is why you may be asked questions that relate to your team working experience during a telephone interview.

There now follows a sample response to this question.

"Yes, I can. I like to keep fit and healthy and as part of this aim I play football for a local Sunday team. We had worked very hard to get to the cup final

and we were faced with playing a very good opposition team who had recently won the league title. After only ten minutes of play, one of our players was sent off and we conceded a penalty as a result. Being one goal down and with 80 minutes left to play, we were faced with a mountain to climb. However, we all remembered our training and worked very hard in order to prevent any more goals being scored. Due to playing with ten players, I had to switch positions and play as a defender, something that I am not used to. The team worked brilliantly to hold off any further opposing goals and after 60 minutes we managed to get an equaliser. The game went to penalties in the end and we managed to win the cup. I believe I am an excellent team player and can always be relied upon to work as an effective team member at all times."

Question 21: Can you provide me with an example of a project you have had to complete and the obstacles you had to overcome?

Having the ability to complete tasks and projects successfully demonstrates that you have the ability to persevere and complete tasks that will form part of your role. Many people give up on things in life and fail to achieve their goals. Any interviewer will want to be convinced that you are going to complete all on-the-job training successfully and, if you can provide evidence of where you have already done this, then this will go in your favour.

When responding to this type of question, try to think of a difficult, drawn out task that you achieved despite a number of obstacles that were in your way. You may choose to use examples from your work life or even from some recent academic work that you have carried out. Take a look at the following sample response:

"Yes I can. I recently successfully completed a NEBOSH course (National Examination Board in Occupational Safety and Health) via distance learning. The course took two years to complete in total and I had to carry out all studying in my own time whilst holding down my current job.

The biggest obstacle I had to overcome was finding the time to complete the work to the high standard that I wanted to achieve. I decided to manage my time effectively and I allocated two hours every evening of the working week in which to complete the work required. I found the time management difficult but I stuck with it and I was determined to complete the course.

In the end I achieved very good results and I very much enjoyed the experience and challenge. I have a determined nature and I have the ability to concentrate for long periods of time when required. I can be relied upon to finish projects to a high standard."

Question 22: What is your sickness record like and what do you think is an acceptable level of sickness?

Most employers detest sickness, and they especially detest sickness that is not genuine. For every day that an employee is off sick, it will cost the company dearly in both financial terms, and also in terms of productivity. Therefore, they want to employ people who have a good sickness record. Obviously you cannot lie when responding to this question, as the company you are applying to join will carry out checks and references.

The latter part of the question is simple to answer. Basically no amount of sickness is acceptable but sometimes genuine sickness cannot be avoided. Remember to tell the interviewer that you do not take time off sick unless absolutely necessary and you can be relied upon to come to work.

Take a look at the following sample response.

"Any form of sickness is not acceptable. However, sometimes people need to go off sick if they are genuinely ill. I would always try my hardest to get into work. If I was ill then I would much prefer it if my line manager sent me home rather than calling in sick. Having said that, I would not want to give a cold or bug to other staff members in the office, as this could have an even worse effect on the company. During the last 12 months I have had only 4 days sickness. These days were for food poisoning, and there was no way I could get out of bed! I fully understand the importance of maintaining a good attendance record and I can always be relied upon not to go off sick unless I am genuinely ill. My previous employer will indicate this in any reference."

Question 23: What are the mission and aims of our company?

Many organisations set themselves aims and objectives. These are sometimes in the form of a vision or charter. They usually relate to the high level of customer service that they promise to deliver. When you apply for any role you should not only prepare for each stage of the selection process but you should also learn as much as possible about the company you are applying to join. Learning this kind of information is important and it will demonstrate your seriousness about joining their particular company. Visit the website of the company you are applying for in order to view their mission, aims, objectives or customer charter.

The following is a sample fictitious customer charter:

DELIVERING QUALITY SERVICE EVERY TIME

The Customer Charter sets out our commitment to delivering a high standard of customer service. It outlines:

- the type of service we aim to provide
- how to contact us and give us feedback, particularly if anything goes wrong, and
- how you can assist us to better serve you

Our goal is to help you achieve what you need by providing quality advice, products and services. We believe that excellent customer relationships are the result of us working together to deliver great outcomes for you by:

- developing trust through open, honest and simple communication
- being approachable and listening to your views
- treating you with fairness and respect
- ensuring ease, expertise and efficiency when you deal with us

---

Question 24: Are you willing to relocate?

This is a difficult question to answer. The interviewer would not normally ask this type of question unless there was a requirement to relocate now or in the future. If there is a potential requirement for you to relocate with the job that you are applying for and you answer the question negatively with a 'no', then there is a good chance that you will not get the job. Therefore, the most appropriate answer in this circumstance would be 'yes', providing that is you actually mean it! It is acceptable, however, to ask questions at the end of the telephone interview about relocation packages or the time that you would be expected to relocate. Most of us do not want to relocate and therefore there should be an incentive for a move.

"Yes I would be willing to relocate and I have already discussed this with my family. Naturally I would like to discuss the relocation package that the company offers if I was to be successful, but I fully appreciate that there may be a need to relocate. If I ever achieved promotion within the company then I would certainly be willing to relocate. I am committed to this job longterm and would do everything within reason to work hard for the company and if that meant being in a different location then I would rise to the challenge. I have had plenty of experience moving around and I know that I could settle into a new environment quickly."

Question 25: Can you tell us about a situation where you demonstrated leadership?

Before we take a look at a sample response to this question, first we need to explore the definition of 'leadership'. A simple definition of leadership is that leadership is the art of motivating a group of people to act towards achieving a common goal. Put even more simply, the leader is the inspiration and director of the action. He or she is the person in the group that possesses the combination of personality and skills that makes others want to follow his or her direction. Ok, now that we understand what leadership means, here is a sample response:

"One evening, at the change of shift, I became aware that two members of the team were late for work. There had been heavy snowfall that day and the congestion on the surrounding roads meant that many people could not get to work. I took it upon myself to lead the team through the coming shift and, despite being two people down, we managed to achieve the goal of providing first class service to our customers. To begin with, I briefed the remainder of the team on the difficulty of the task that lay ahead of us. I assessed the skill levels and experience within the team and allocated tasks accordingly. I ensured that I remained confident and in control during the brief so that the team members would have confidence in my ability to manage the problem. As the shift progressed I had a number of different problems to deal with but I remained calm, listened

carefully to the problems, and directed accordingly. At the end of the shift we congratulated ourselves on a job well done and discussed the areas in which we felt we could improve, if the same situation was to arise again."

Question 26: Can you explain the difference between a manager and a leader?

The difference between a manager and a leader can be summed up as follows:

It is a manager's responsibility to make effective use of the resources that are at his/her disposal. This may include planning ahead, ensuring there are sufficient resources available, and making the best use of their teams skills, strengths and qualities. A leader will use his or her skills and experiences to motivate the team and direct them towards the desired goal. All good leaders will be visionaries who have one eye on the end target.

Keywords used to describe the functions of a manager

- Planning
- Effective use of resources
- Strategic thinking
- Organising

Keywords used to describe the functions of a leader

- Visionary
- Motivator
- Inspiring

If you can provide specific examples in your response where you have demonstrated leadership skills and also management skills then even better!

Question 27: What makes a good leader?

In order to become a good leader you must have a number of different skills that you can draw upon at a moment's notice and these include:

Being a visionary – An ability to see the end result or the desired goal.

Provide inspiration – Great leaders need to be capable of inspiring their team towards a goal or objective.

Strategic thinker – Being able to think outside of the box and plan for the future.

Being liked by the team – Whilst not essential, it certainly helps to be liked by your team. If they like you, the will follow you.

Being an effective decision maker – Having the ability to make decisions, even sometimes unpopular ones.

Accepting of feedback and criticism – Good leaders should be able to take criticism from others. This will help them to continually improve.

Whilst the above list is not exhaustive, it will provide you with a number of useful tips that will assist you during your preparation.

Question 28: What has been your biggest failure to date?

Now, this really is a difficult question to answer! Get this wrong and it could be all over. The majority of people will answer this question in the following manner:

"To be honest, I don't normally fail at anything. I prepare so well for everything that I do that success is inevitable."

Well, if you answer it in this style then you are probably about to just fail your first big thing – your interview!

Everybody makes mistakes. Everybody fails at something. It's what you do about the failure that's the important part. Take a look at the following sample response:

"I would say my biggest failure to date is failing an educational course that I embarked upon approximately two years ago. The reason why I failed the course was primarily due to a lack of adequate time set aside for studying. However, I immediately learnt from my mistakes and shortcomings and I booked to re-sit the test immediately. I worked hard during the build up to the re-sit and I spent lots of time studying. I passed the test with flying colours. I certainly learnt a lot from my initial failure and I always make sure that I now prepare fully for everything that I do."

Question 29: Do you need other people around to stimulate you, or are you self-motivated?

Most employers want their staff to be self-motivated. If an employee is self-motivated then he or she are going to perform to a high standard. Having personally employed people in the past, I find that those individuals who are self-motivated will do a good job for me. They will find things to do when it is quiet, and they will also be motivated by their own success and achievements at work. Whilst pay is a motivating factor for an employee, it is not the most important. Job satisfaction is vital if a person is going to perform well at work.

Your response to this question during the telephone interview should focus on providing examples of where you have been self-motivated in a current or previous work role. It is easy for an interviewee to say that they are self-motivated, but proving it with examples is a different matter.

Take a look at the following sample response:

"Whilst I enjoy working in a team environment I am a highly self-motivated person. I don't like it when I'm sat around doing nothing, so I'm always on the look out for new things to do. That applies to when I'm either at home or at work. For example, during my last job when we were going through a quiet spell, I wanted to look for ways to improve the company turnover. Without being asked I set about researching different areas that the company could potentially draw more income streams from. I contacted a number of potential customers and arranged to send them some company literature and sample products. From this work I managed to created six new leads for the company and my manager was very pleased with the fact that I'd been self-motivated enough to try to make a positive difference."

Question 30: Are you accepted into a team quickly?

Remember that teamwork is very important in the vast majority of organisations. Therefore, being able to fit into a team environment will be a positive thing. Again, I would advise that you try to think of examples where you have previously joined a new team, and adapted quickly.

Take a look at the following sample response:

"I am inherently a great team player, so the answer to this question would have to be a definite yes. I have worked in lots or teams in the past and

this is usually when I am at my best. I understand that when you join a new team you need to fit into the new environment and make an effort to introduce yourself, get to know the people in the team and also how the team operates. I believe that, by understanding the key elements of a team, I am capable of quickly being accepted in the vast majority of teams. Team members need to be good communicators, listeners, supporters and motivators. Each team needs a variety of different skill-sets and I believe I have lots of qualities to bring to any team environment.

Whilst working for a previous employer I was required to join a new team because a lady had gone on maternity leave. I quickly assessed the dynamics of the team and tried to fit in as best that I could. Because I was so adaptable, each member of the team welcomed me and helped me to get settled in quickly. I understand that if I am successful then I will be required to quickly adapt to the team environment. This will not be a problem for me and I am in fact looking forward to the new challenge."

Question 31: What do you think the qualities of a good team player are?

Having knowledge of how a team operates and the qualities required to become a competent team player would be an advantage before you undertake your telephone interview. Take a look at the following 'team' qualities:

- An ability to interact and work with others, regardless of their age, sex, religion, sexual orientation, background, disability or appearance;
- Being able to communicate with everyone in the team and provide the appropriate level of support and encouragement;
- Being capable of carrying out tasks correctly, professionally and in accordance with guidelines and regulations;
- Being focused on the team's goal(s);
- Having a flexible attitude and approach to the task;
- Putting the needs of the team first before your own;
- Putting personal differences aside for the sake of the team;
- Being able to listen to others' suggestions and contributions.

When responding to this type of question it would be an advantage if you could back up your response with an example of where you have already work in a team. Take a look at the following sample response:

"A good team player must have many different qualities including an ability to listen carefully to a given brief. If you don't listen to the brief that is provided then you can't complete the task properly. In addition to listening carefully to the brief you must be able to communicate effectively with everyone in the team. This will include providing support for the other team members and also listening to other people's suggestions on how a task can be achieved. You also have to be able to work with anyone in the team regardless of their age, background, religion, sexual orientation, disability or appearance. You can't discriminate against anyone and if you do, then there is no place for you within that team. A good team player must also be able to carry out his or her job professionally and competently. When I say competently I mean correctly and in accordance with guidelines and training. You should also be focused on the team's goal and not be distracted by any external factors. Putting the needs of the team first is paramount. Finally a good team player must be flexible and be able to adapt to the changing requirements of the team.

I already have some experience of working in a team and I know how important it is to work hard at achieving the task. In a previous job we would have a weekly team briefing. During the team briefings my manager would inform us what jobs need to be carried out as a priority. During one particular meeting he asked three of us to clear a fire escape that had become blocked with cardboard boxes, debris and rubbish. He also asked us to come up with a plan to prevent it from happening again. We quickly set about the task carefully removing the rubbish and I had the responsibility of arranging for a refuse collection company to come and dispose of the rubbish. We also had to work together to find ways of preventing the rubbish from being haphazardly disposed in the same way again in the future. We sat down together and wrote out a memorandum for our manager that he could distribute to all staff. At the end of the job we'd worked well to achieve the task and no more rubbish was ever disposed in the fire escape again. My manager was very pleased with the job we'd done."

Question 32: Can you tell me about any achievements you have experienced during your life so far?

Those people who can demonstrate a history of achievement are far more likely to continue to succeed in their new working environment. Having achieved something in your life demonstrates that you have the ability to see things through to the end, something that is crucial to your new career. It also shows that you are motivated and determined to succeed. Try to think of examples where you have succeeded or achieved something relevant in your life. Some good examples of achievements are as follows:

- Winning a trophy with a football or hockey team;
- GCSEs and other educational qualifications;
- Duke of Edinburgh's Award;
- Being given responsibility at work or at school;
- Raising money for charity.

"Yes I can. So far in my life I have achieved quite a few things that I am proud of. To begin with I achieved good grades whilst at school including a grade 'A' in English. I worked very hard to achieve my grades and I'm proud of them. At weekends I play rugby for a local team and I've achieved a number of things with them. Apart from winning the league last year we also held a charity match against the local Police rugby team. We managed to raise £500 for a local charity, which was a great achievement. More recently I managed to achieve a huge increase in my fitness levels. I have learnt that you have to work hard in life if you want to achieve things and I have a positive attitude to hard work. My own personal motto is 'work hard and you'll be rewarded'."

Question 33: What is the best example of customer service you have come across?

This type of question is designed to see how high your standards are, in relation to customer service. Try to think of an occasion when you have witnessed an excellent piece of customer service and show that you learned from it. If you are very confident, then you may have an occasion when you, yourself, provided that service. Whatever response you provide, make sure it is unique and stands out.

"Whilst working as a shop assistant in my current role, a member of the public came in to complain to the manager about a pair of football shoes that he had bought for his son's birthday. When his son came to open the present on the morning of his birthday, he noticed that one of the football boots was a larger size than the other. He was supposed to be playing football with his friends that morning and wanted to wear his new boots. However, due to the shop's mistake, this was not possible. Naturally, the boy was very upset. The manager of the shop was excellent in her approach to dealing with situation. She remained calm throughout and listened to the gentleman very carefully, showing complete empathy for his son's situation. This immediately diffused any potential confrontation. She then told him how sorry she was for the mistake that had happened, and that she would feel exactly the same if it was her own son who it had happened to. She then told the gentleman that she would refund the money in full and give his son a new pair of football boots to the same value as the previous pair. The man was delighted with her offer. Not only that, she then offered to give the man a further discount of 10% on any future purchase, due to the added inconvenience that was caused by him having to return to the shop to sort out the problem. I learned a lot from the way my manager dealt with this situation. She used exceptional communication skills and remained calm throughout. She then went the extra mile to make the gentleman's journey back to the shop a worthwhile one. The potential for losing a customer was averted by her actions and I felt sure the man would return to our shop again."

Question 34: What do you dislike doing in a work environment?

Be very careful how you respond to this type of question. The things that you dislike should be totally disassociated with any elements of the job you are applying for. For example, if you are applying for a job that is primarily customer-focused, don't tell the panel that you dislike dealing with people's problems or queries. If you are applying for an office job, don't tell the interviewer that you dislike being sat behind a desk all day. You should also avoid responses that portray yourself as a person who is not self-motivated. I can remember asking this question to an applicant during an interview and he replied with:

"I don't like having nothing to do. I get bored if there's not much to do in the office. I enjoy being busy at work and I like to be kept active."

On the face of it, this doesn't appear to be a bad response. However, a person who is sat around doing nothing should be looking for other things to do whilst at work. There are always things to do in a working environment, whether that's organising the following days work, or even asking fellow colleagues if they need help with any element of their own work.

"There's nothing in particular that I dislike doing in a working environment. Whilst I like to be kept active, if I have completed all of my work for the day, then I will always look for other things to do, or even offer to help a work colleague with their work. Sometimes at work we have to carry out monotonous and repetitive tasks. Whilst these aren't my favourite parts of the working day, I always carry them out diligently and professionally."

Question 35: What salary are you looking for?

This can be a very tricky question to answer. Everybody wants to earn the highest salary possible; yet at the same time you do not want to come across as either arrogant or overconfident. The key to answering this question is to make sure you justify the salary that you are after.

Personally, when responding to this question, I will always go for the highest salary possible. I do this with the thinking that I can always come down a little if they decide that they don't want to pay me what I believe I am worth. Remember that you only get one chance to provide a figure. If that figure is low, then there's no way that you'll be able to negotiate an increased amount. Be confident and be comfortable with the amount that you want.

Sample response based on a wage band of £17,000 – £24,000

"I would like a salary of £23,500 per annum. The reason why I would like this amount is simply because I have the skills, qualifications and experience to perform exceptionally in the role. Even though I believe I am worth £24,000, I would much prefer to start on a lower scale and prove to you how good I am. I feel very strongly that you'll be pleased with my performance and that I am worth this salary. Although money is not the main motivating factor for me, I do believe that I am worth this amount."

The above sample response displays a level of confidence that the employer will find appealing. However, if you say you are good at a job, then you will need to prove this during your initial probationary period.

Question 36: What didn't you like about your last job?

If you are applying to move jobs into an external company then there will obviously be a reason why you want to move. We all have bad experiences in the working environment, and more often than not, the majority of people want to move simply because that either don't like their boss, or the people that they work with. Whatever you do, do not be disrespectful to any of your previous managers or work colleagues, no matter how much you disliked them! You should also avoid using salary as a motivating factor for moving jobs. I have heard some horror responses to this question during my time as an interviewer. Here's one of them:

"To be honest, I don't get on well with my boss. He treats me poorly and everyone in the office thinks he's a bully."

Whilst I didn't doubt the person's claims, I believe that any grievances should be kept to yourself. The key to answering this question successfully is to choose a genuine reason that shows you are motivated, and also that you want a new and fresh challenge.

"Basically I am ready for a new challenge. I have been in my previous role for seven years now and I feel the time has come for me to move on. I get on very well with my manager and all of the members in my team. Whilst I will miss them, I don't feel that I can develop any further in the same position. I am applying for this new job, as I believe I can offer a great deal in terms of my skills and experiences. I am really looking forward to a new challenge and the benefits of working in a brand new environment."

Question 37: I presume that you have read the job description, so therefore which areas of the job appeal to you the least?

During an earlier section of this guide I explained how important it is to read and study the job description and person specification for the job. This question is one of the reasons why you must do just that! If you don't know what is contained within these important documents, then not only should you not be applying for the job, you'll also have no hope of answering the question.

Most telephone interviewers will assess you against the job description. The job description is basically a blueprint for the role that you are applying for and it determines the skills and attributes required to perform the job competently. Make sure you read the job description and also have examples ready of where you match each assessable area.

"Yes I have been studying the job description for some time now. To be honest, there aren't any elements that I wouldn't find appealing. To begin with, the requirement to deal with customers' queries and complaints is something that I would very much enjoy. I get a lot of satisfaction out of helping people so this would not be a problem for me. The part in the description that requires you to respond quickly to queries, again is not an issue. I am very organised and always complete tasks at the soonest opportunity. I also understand that there is a requirement for me to record details of every telephone call that I handle. This is fundamental to the role as it is important to keep a track of progress when dealing with customers' issues. Again, this would not be a problem for me simply because I enjoy being organised. As mentioned already, there are no elements of the job description that I would dislike. I have carefully studied all elements and would relish the opportunity to work in this role."

Question 38: What do you think of your current company?

Whilst this question is primarily aimed at assessing the reasons why you are wishing to leave your current employer, it also assesses how mature and professional you are as an employee. Regardless of what you truly think about your current employer, never be critical of them to others, especially during a telephone or normal interview. If you are critical of your previous employer during the interview, then there is strong chance that you could be critical of this new employer once you have started! Remember to always be professional during your responses to interview questions and never respond to questions based on your personal feelings.

The key to responding to this question correctly is to state that your previous employer gave you many different skills that would be of benefit to your potential new employer. Your current employer's loss if your next employer's gain.

"I think they are great. I've had a wonderful time with them over the last few years. They have been very supportive of me and helped me to develop both personally and professionally. They are a well-respected employer and I believe that the skills I have learnt from them will benefit me, and also the next organisation that I work for, which will hopefully be yours. Even though

I have had a great time working for them, I am personally ready for a new challenge, which is why I am here today."

Question 39: I see from your application form that you have only been with your current employer for six months. Why do you want to move so soon?

This again is quite a tricky question to answer. I have looked at a person's CV and application form before I undertake the telephone interview, and have often wondered why they want to move jobs so soon after joining. In order to convince me they need to have a very good response to this question.

Of course, the probable reason why someone wants to move so soon is because they are unhappy in their job. If this is really the case, then I would much rather if the person was honest. Take a look at the following response, which was very similar to a person's response after I had asked this exact question:

"I have to be honest here; the job that I joined isn't what I expected. Whilst the employer is very good, the job has turned out to be different than the one advertised. I applied to become a sales representative, which is where my strengths are, but the job has ended up being an office-based role that requires me to primarily deal with customer queries. Whilst I don't mind doing this, it isn't the job that I applied for or the one that was sold to me when I applied. I could sit here and give you other reasons why I want to move on so quickly, but it is important that I am honest. I want you to know that I am not the kind or person who jumps from job to job and I feel certain that my current employer will give me a glowing reference. I am looking for a stable job that is suited to my skills and experiences, and the one I am applying for today certainly fits that description perfectly."

Question 40: I see there have been some gaps in your employment. Can you explain these?

If you have had any gaps in your employment then it is advisable that you have a valid reason for them. When responding to this type of question try to provide beneficial reasons for the gaps. Some good reasons for gaps in employment might be:

- Taking time off work to complete a study of development course
- Travelling to develop yourself or learn about a different language or culture
- Helping sick relatives or friends
- Carrying out voluntary work or community work

However, some not so good reasons for gaps in employment are:

- Getting over a previous stressful job
- Going on holiday with your friends
- You fancied a break from employment all together

The above will most probably put off a potential employer as there is a strong chance that you might want to leave them for a further gap in your employment.

"I took six months out from work to concentrate on finishing my Diploma educational course. I was eager to gain good grades so I decided to take a gap in my employment to fulfill this desire. It turned out to be a very good choice as I achieved excellent grades."

Question 41: Do you have any questions for me?

You've reached the end of the telephone interview and the interviewer will now ask you a question similar to the above. How do you answer it without ruining your chances of success? I know of people who have ruined their interview, simply by asking irrelevant and arrogant questions at the end. Be careful what you ask the interviewer and, if you do decide to ask questions, keep them to a minimum or two or three and ask questions that the interviewer can easily answer.

Take a look at the following sample responses:

"Yes I just have one question please. If I am to be successful, how soon would it be before I start?" **This displays a level of enthusiasm.**

"I noticed on your website whilst carrying out my research that you have been running a campaign aimed at attracting more customers to your website. Has this been a success?" **This displays an enthusiastic interest in their company and the fact that you have carried out some research.**

"I appreciate that I am yet to find out whether or not I am successful, but is there anything I can read to prepare myself for the job, just in case I am successful?" **This displays motivation and conscientiousness.**

"I notice that you have introduced a new exciting product range. Has this been a success?" **This displays an enthusiastic interest in their company and the fact that you have carried out some research.**

FINAL SAMPLE TELEPHONE INTERVIEW QUESTIONS WITH TIPS ON ANSWERING THEM

In this final section I will provide you with some questions I have found during my research that have been asked during telephone interviews. I have also provided a few tips after each one to help you answer them effectively.

Q. Why do you want to work for our organisation?

Tell them about the positive things you've learnt during your research. If they have won any awards, or if they have been in the news for good reasons, try to include these in your response. You may also choose to tell them that you have heard positive things about the company during your research.

Q. Why do you want to work in the job you have applied for?

The best way to respond to this question is to tell them that you have studied the role carefully and that you have the skills to match it. You also believe that the role is one that you can excel in and you can bring something positive to their organisation.

Q. What qualities are important to work in the role you are applying for?

Simply tell them the qualities you have learnt whilst researching the person specification and job description.

Q. What evidence can you give to show you possess these qualities?

When answering this question come up with examples that match the person specification. For example, if one of the qualities is that of 'customer service', tell them a specific example of where you have already carried out this work in a previous role. Remember also to use the STAR method when answering the question.

Q. What do we do?

Visit their website and don't forget to learn their mission, values and goals.

Q. Tell me about a time when you have had to cope with pressure?

Again, use the STAR method when responding. You should also state that, in situations like these, you remain calm and focused on achieving the task in hand.

Q. Tell me about a challenge you have faced. How did you conduct the challenge?

This could be a tough question to answer. However, if you use the STAR method when responding to it, you will answer it in a concise and appropriate manner. You should always try to ensure that there is a positive outcome to the challenge you undertook. Here is a really great response to this question:

"I was working at a restaurant and noticed a divide between the waiters and kitchen staff. Most of the kitchen staff were older than their waiter colleagues and they had migrated from India. There was very little interaction between the kitchen and waiter staff colleagues and I was concerned that this barrier would not only make the kitchen staff feel isolated, but that it would also have a negative impact on the team environment. I decided to take on the challenge of improving working relations.

My initial considerations were to ensure that the kitchen staff felt comfortable and that they could also speak to me and the waiters if they needed help or assistance. After all, they had not been in the country for long and I wanted them to feel welcome and valued. I believe that communication between colleagues within a workplace is essential to achieve the best possible results and create a good working environment, regardless of individual differences.

To overcome the challenges I introduced myself to all the kitchen staff members and I learnt their names. This ensured that they felt valued and that they also had a point of contact if they ever needed assistance or support. I also encouraged the other waiters to communicate with their kitchen colleagues. Following my actions communication improved and the workplace is now a more efficient and happier working environment."

Q. Describe a time when you had to deal with a difficult customer?

In the vast majority of roles you will be required to provide excellent customer service. Here is a great response to this question.

"Whilst working as a shop assistant in my current role, a member of the public came in to complain about a pair of football shoes that he had bought for his son's birthday. When his son came to open the present on the morning of his birthday, he noticed that one of the football boots was a larger size than the other. He was supposed to be playing football with his

friends that morning and wanted to wear his new boots. However, due to the shop's mistake, this was not possible. Naturally, the boy was very upset and the customer was very angry.

I remained calm throughout and listened to the gentleman very carefully, showing complete empathy for his son's situation. This immediately defused any potential confrontation. I then told him how sorry I was for the mistake that had happened, and that I would feel exactly the same, if it was my own son who this had happened to. I then told the gentleman that I would refund the money in full and give his son a new pair of football boots to the same value as the previous pair. The man was delighted with my offer. I then offered to give the man a further discount of 10% on any future purchase, due to the added inconvenience that was caused by him having to return to the shop to sort out the problem. The potential for losing a customer was averted by my actions and I feel sure the man would return to our shop again."

Q. How would you deal with a customer complaint?

Dealing with and resolving a customer complaint is all part and parcel of everyday working life in certain industries. I want to spend a little bit of time teaching you the most effective way to deal with complaints. This will then enable you to answer the questions correctly.

In any industry or profession where a customer is complaining, there are a number of key areas that the complainant is concerned with:

- They want someone to **listen** to their complaint.
- They want someone to **understand** why they are complaining.
- They want someone to **sort out** their complaint as soon as possible.
- They would like an **apology**.
- They want someone to **explain** what has gone wrong.

When dealing with customer complaints in any form, you will need to follow an action plan. This action plan is explained in detail on the following pages. Whilst I haven't provided you with a specific response to this question, the following information and guidance will help you to answer it sufficiently.

The plan follows a structured format and each area follows on systematically from the other. To begin with, you will listen to the complaint using effective verbal and nonverbal listening skills. The majority of people associate communication skills primarily with the spoken word. However, these cover a number of areas. Having the ability to actively listen is a key factor to resolving the complaint successfully. Take a look at the stages of dealing with complaints before reading each individual section.

LISTEN TO THE COMPLAINT

↓

APOLOGISE AND APPRECIATE

↓

GATHER INFORMATION

↓

PROVIDE A SOLUTION

↓

REACH AN AGREEMENT

↓

TAKE ACTION

↓

FOLLOW UP

LISTEN TO THE COMPLAINT

One of the most important factors, when dealing with the complaint, is to listen. Listening effectively can be done in a number of ways. This can be achieved through facial expression, body language, oral confirmation and clarification techniques. Maintain good eye contact throughout, nod, use an interested facial expression and confirm back to the customer what they have told you. If they begin to shout, become aggressive or confrontational, or even start swearing, then you will have to be assertive in your response and inform them that their language will not be tolerated. Inform them that you want to deal with their complaint quickly and to their satisfaction, but it must be done in a calm manner.

APOLOGISE AND APPRECIATE

Once you have listened to their complaint, you need to apologise and explain that you fully understand how they feel. This will usually have the effect of defusing any confrontation and will make the complainant feel that they are being heard. It is all about establishing a rapport with the passenger and making them feel that their complaint is important.

The following is a sample response to a customer's complaint:

"Thank you for taking the time, sir, to explain what the problem is. If the same situation had happened to me I would certainly feel as you do."

In just two sentences, you have made the complainant feel valued and understood. Now you can begin to resolve the issue and you will find it easier to talk to them from now on.

Providing their complaint is genuine, you should now take ownership of the complaint and see it through to a successful resolution. You have listened to their complaint and acknowledged there is an issue. Now move on to establishing the facts, which will give you the tools to create a successful resolution.

GATHER INFORMATION

When dealing with a complaint the next important stage is to gather as much essential information as possible. The reason for doing this is that it will allow you to make a more informed judgement about the situation and it will also allow you to take steps to prevent it from happening again.

Complaints take time to deal with and detract you from other important duties. When a member of the team is dealing with a complaint, the rest of team must make up for the deficit in numbers. Therefore, if the situation that led to the complaint in the first instance can be avoided in the future, this will help the organisation to provide a better service. When gathering information, concentrate on the following areas:

- What is the complaint in relation to?
- What are the facts of the incident?
- Who was responsible?
- How would the customer like the problem to be resolved?

Once you have gathered all of the facts, you will then be able to take action to resolve the issue.

PROVIDE A SOLUTION

Coming up with a suitable solution to the customer's complaint can be difficult, especially if they are reluctant to accept any reasonable offering. Therefore, it is important that you remain calm throughout. Make sure that the solution/s you offer are relevant to the situation and are achievable. If they are not, then do not make the mistake of offering something you cannot deliver. This will just make the situation worse. When providing a solution, ask the customer if your offer is acceptable. By offering different solutions to the complainant you are asking them to make the decision for you, and therefore making your life easier. This way, they will end up getting what they want and, therefore, will be happy with the resolution.

Remember – when dealing with the complaint, never take it personally and never be rude or confrontational.

REACH AN AGREEMENT

Once you have offered the solution, make sure you get the complainants approval first. This will prevent them from complaining about the action you are taking to resolve the issue. The most effective method of achieving this is through verbal acknowledgement.

Reaching an agreement is important psychologically. The customer will feel that you are being considerate to their needs and, by reaffirming the solution with them; you are showing them that you have their interests at heart.

TAKE ACTION

Plain and simple. Now that you have reached an agreement, get on with task in hand. If it is going to take you a while to take the action agreed upon, you might find it useful to inform the passenger.

You have now reached the end of the guide and I sincerely hope that you have found it a useful resource in helping you to prepare for your telephone interview.

If you have access to the internet then I would now recommend you take the time to watch my telephone interview training videos at the following website:

WWW.INTERVIEW-TRAINING-ONLINE.CO.UK

Good luck,
Richard McMunn

how2become

Visit www.how2become.com to find
more titles and courses that will
help you to pass any job interview or
selection process:

• Online psychometric testing

• Job interview DVDs and books

• 1-day intensive career training courses

• Psychometric testing books and CDs

www.how2become.com